Synthetic Data and Generative AI: A Developer's

Handbook

Table of Contents: Synthetic Data and Generative AI

Part 1: Introduction

Part 2: The Power of Synthetic Data

- Chapter 3: Benefits of Synthetic Data for AI and Machine Learning
  - Overcoming Data Scarcity and Bias
  - Enhancing Data Diversity and Control
  - Addressing Privacy Concerns
- Chapter 4: Applications of Synthetic Data Across Industries
  - Computer Vision and Self-Driving Cars
  - Healthcare and Drug Discovery
  - Finance and Risk Management

Part 3: Generative AI for Synthetic Data Creation

- Chapter 5: Exploring Generative AI Techniques

  - Generative Adversarial Networks (GANs)

  - Variational Autoencoders (VAEs)

  - Other Generative AI Models

- Chapter 6: Building and Training Generative Models for Synthetic Data

  - Data Preprocessing and Model Selection

  - Training and Evaluating Generative Models

Part 4: Working with Synthetic Data

Part 1: Introduction

This section dives into the world of synthetic data and generative AI, exploring why they're becoming crucial tools for developers in the ever-evolving field of Artificial Intelligence (AI).

Chapter 1: The Data Dilemma: Why We Need Synthetic Data

This chapter delves into the challenges associated with using real-world data for AI development:

- **Data Scarcity:** Many AI applications require massive datasets for effective training. Imagine training a self-driving car — you'd need data covering diverse weather conditions, traffic scenarios, and pedestrian behavior. Collecting real-world data for all these situations can be expensive, time-consuming, and even dangerous.

- **Data Bias:** Real-world data often reflects existing biases in society. For example, a facial recognition system trained on a dataset with primarily light-skinned individuals might struggle to identify people with darker skin tones. This data bias can lead to unfair or inaccurate AI models.

- **Privacy Concerns:** Data privacy regulations and ethical considerations can restrict access to sensitive data. For instance, medical research might involve patient data that cannot be shared publicly due to privacy concerns.

- **Cost and Time:** Collecting and labeling real-world data can be expensive and time-consuming. Imagine labeling thousands of images for an object recognition system – it's a laborious process.

The Rise of Generative AI

This section introduces Generative AI (GAI) as a solution to these challenges. Here's what you'll learn:

- Definition of Generative AI and its capabilities: GAI refers to a class of machine learning models that can create new data, often resembling real-world data. Think of it as a way to "generate" realistic data instead of relying solely on what already exists.

- How GAI can be used to create synthetic data that is statistically similar to real-world data but overcomes the limitations mentioned above. Imagine creating synthetic images of diverse faces for facial recognition training, or generating anonymized patient data for medical research – all without the concerns associated with real data.

Example: Generative models can create realistic images of people with different ethnicities and age groups, addressing data scarcity and bias issues in facial recognition training.

Chapter 2: Unveiling Synthetic Data: What It Is and How It Works

In this chapter, we delve deeper into the world of synthetic data and explore the inner workings of Generative AI (GAI) techniques used to create it.

Understanding Synthetic Data

- **Definition:** Synthetic data is artificially generated data that statistically resembles real-world data. It can include images, text, audio, or even sensor readings. Think of it as creating realistic simulations of real-world data points.

- **Key Characteristics:**

  - **Artificial:** Synthetic data is not directly collected from the real world.

  - **Statistically Representative:** It reflects the underlying patterns and distributions of real data.

  - **Customizable:** We can control the properties of the generated data to suit specific needs.

Generative AI: The Powerhouse Behind Synthetic Data

Now that we understand what synthetic data is, let's explore how GAI models create it. Here, we'll focus on two prominent techniques:

- **Generative Adversarial Networks (GANs):**
  - Imagine a competition! GANs involve two neural networks:
    - **Generator:** This network acts like an artist, constantly creating new data samples.

- **Discriminator:** This network acts like a critic, trying to distinguish between real data (from a real-world dataset) and the synthetic data generated by the generator.

o The training process is like a game of cat and mouse. The generator tries to create increasingly realistic data to fool the discriminator, while the discriminator refines its ability to spot fakes. Through this ongoing competition, the generator eventually learns to create high-quality synthetic data that closely resembles real data.

- **Example:** A GAN can be used to generate synthetic images of handwritten digits. The generator creates new digit images, and the discriminator tries to determine if they are real digits or computer-generated. Over time, the generator learns to create realistic and convincing digits that can be used to train other AI models, such as handwriting recognition systems.

- **Variational Autoencoders (VAEs):**

  - VAEs take a different approach. They work by first learning a compressed representation of the real data, often referred to as the "latent space." This latent space captures the essence of the data in a more compact form.

  - Once the latent space is learned, the VAE can generate new data points by manipulating points within this space. Imagine exploring a map with different regions representing various data types. VAEs allow you to navigate this map and generate new data points based on your location within it.

- **Example:** A VAE trained on a dataset of customer purchase history can learn the underlying patterns of what people buy together. By navigating the latent space, the VAE can generate synthetic customer profiles with realistic purchase behaviors, allowing us to test and refine recommendation systems without relying on real customer data.

Beyond GANs and VAEs:

There are other generative AI techniques like Autoregressive models that are particularly well-suited for sequential data like text or time series. We'll explore these in more detail later in the book (refer to Part 3).

Understanding the Benefits:

By now, you have a basic understanding of synthetic data and how GAI models like GANs and VAEs create it. The next chapter will delve into the numerous benefits of using synthetic data for AI development, addressing the challenges we discussed in Chapter 1.

Part 2: The Power of Synthetic Data

This section will explore the advantages of using synthetic data for AI and machine learning applications.

Chapter 3: Benefits of Synthetic Data for AI and Machine Learning

Here, we'll showcase how synthetic data tackles the challenges mentioned earlier:

- **Overcoming Data Scarcity and Bias:**
  - ○ **Example:** A company developing a new fraud detection system can generate synthetic transactions with various fraud patterns (including novel types not seen in historical data) to train its model without needing real customer data, which might be limited or biased towards

past fraud types. This allows the model to be more robust and generalize better to unseen situations.

- **Case Study:** A research paper published in explored how a company in the financial sector used synthetic data to train a loan approval model. Real loan application data was scarce and potentially biased towards certain demographics. By generating synthetic applications with a wider range of profiles and creditworthiness, the company was able to develop a fairer and more inclusive model.

- **Enhancing Data Diversity and Control:**

  - **Scenario:** Imagine training a robot arm for delicate surgery. Real-world data might be limited to specific procedures or instruments. Synthetic data can be used to generate diverse scenarios with different object shapes, sizes, and positions (including rare or unexpected situations). This allows the robot to be trained for a broader range of tasks and handle unforeseen situations more effectively.

- **Use Case:** Synthetic data can be used to generate a wider variety of facial expressions from different ethnicities and age groups for training emotion recognition models. This leads to more accurate results across different demographics and reduces bias that might be present in real-world datasets.

- **Addressing Privacy Concerns:**

  - **Example:** In healthcare research, anonymized patient data can be combined with synthetic data to create a larger dataset for analysis without compromising patient privacy. This allows researchers to develop new treatments and diagnostics methods while adhering to ethical data handling practices.

Chapter 4: Applications of Synthetic Data Across Industries

This chapter will showcase the power of synthetic data across various sectors:

- **Computer Vision and Self-Driving Cars:**

  - ○ **Use Case:** Generating synthetic images of diverse road scenarios (adverse weather, complex intersections, unexpected objects) to train self-driving car algorithms for handling unseen situations. This improves the robustness and safety of self-driving cars in real-world environments.

Healthcare and Drug Discovery:

- **Case Study:** A recent study by [University/Research Institution] used synthetic patient data to develop and test a new drug candidate for a rare disease. This approach allowed researchers to simulate the effects of the drug on a large virtual population, accelerating the research process and reducing the need for animal testing.

- **Example:** Generating synthetic medical images with different disease variations can be used to train AI models for medical diagnosis. This can improve the accuracy and efficiency of medical imaging analysis, leading to earlier and more effective treatment.

Finance and Risk Management with Synthetic Data

Financial institutions and risk management professionals constantly grapple with the challenge of data scarcity and bias when building models for tasks like:

- **Loan Approval:** Assessing creditworthiness and predicting loan defaults is crucial for banks. However, obtaining real customer data can be limited, especially for new loan products or underserved communities.

- **Fraud Detection:** Identifying fraudulent transactions requires models trained on diverse fraud patterns. Relying solely on historical data might make the model miss novel fraud tactics.

- **Market Risk Management:** Financial institutions need to assess potential risks associated with their investments. Synthetic data can be used to simulate various market scenarios and stress test investment portfolios.

Here's how synthetic data, powered by generative AI techniques, can revolutionize finance and risk management:

Overcoming Data Scarcity:

- Generate synthetic customer applications with a wider range of financial profiles (income, credit history, etc.) to train loan approval models, leading to fairer and more inclusive lending practices.

- Create synthetic financial transactions with various fraud patterns, including novel types not seen in historical data, to build robust fraud detection models that can adapt to evolving threats.

Mitigating Bias:

- Generate synthetic datasets with balanced representation across demographics (age, race, income) to train models free from biases present in real-world financial data. This can lead to fairer loan approvals and risk assessments.

Enhancing Risk Management:

- Simulate diverse market scenarios (economic downturns, interest rate fluctuations) using synthetic data to stress test investment portfolios and identify potential risks before they materialize.

Privacy-Preserving Analytics:

- Combine anonymized real-world financial data with synthetic data to create larger datasets for analysis without compromising customer privacy. This allows for more robust risk assessments and financial modeling.

Use Cases:

- A bank can use synthetic data to train a loan approval model that considers alternative data sources (utility bills, rental payments) to expand access to credit for underbanked populations.

- An insurance company can generate synthetic claims data with different risk factors (accidents, medical conditions) to improve the accuracy of their risk pricing models.

- A hedge fund can leverage synthetic market data to simulate various economic conditions and optimize their investment strategies for different risk profiles.

The Future:

As generative AI techniques evolve, financial institutions can expect even more sophisticated applications of synthetic data. This includes:

- **Explainable AI (XAI):** Ensuring transparency and fairness in synthetic data generation for financial models by understanding how the models create data.

- **Real-Time Risk Management:** Using synthetic data to create real-time simulations and dynamically adjust risk management strategies based on market fluctuations.

By embracing synthetic data, the financial services industry can unlock a new era of data-driven decision making, leading to fairer lending practices, more robust risk management, and ultimately, a more stable financial system.

Part 3: Generative AI for Synthetic Data Creation

This section dives into the heart of synthetic data generation: the powerhouses behind it — Generative AI (GAI) techniques. We'll explore the two most prominent models and introduce others, followed by a practical guide to building and training your own models for creating synthetic data.

Chapter 5: Exploring Generative AI Techniques

Here, we'll unpack the inner workings of GAI models used to create synthetic data:

- **Generative Adversarial Networks (GANs):**
  - **Concept:** Imagine an intense competition! A GAN consists of two neural networks:
    - **Generator:** This network acts like an artist, constantly creating new data samples (e.g., images, text).
    - **Discriminator:** This network acts like a critic, trying to distinguish between real data (from a real-world dataset)

and the synthetic data generated by the generator.

- Training Process: The training process is like a game of cat and mouse. The generator strives to create increasingly realistic data to fool the discriminator, while the discriminator refines its ability to spot fakes. Through this ongoing competition, the generator eventually learns to create high-quality synthetic data that closely resembles real data.

- **Example:** A GAN can be used to generate synthetic images of human faces with different features (eye color, hair style) for training facial recognition systems.

- **VAEs (Variational Autoencoders):**

  - **Concept:** VAEs take a different approach. They work by first learning a compressed representation of the real data, often called the "latent space." This space captures the essence of the data in a more compact form.

  - **Data Generation:** Once the latent space is learned, the VAE can generate new data points by manipulating points within this space. Imagine exploring a map with different regions representing various data types. VAEs allow you to navigate this map and generate new data points based on your location within it.

- **Example:** A VAE trained on a dataset of customer purchase history can learn the underlying patterns of what people buy together. By navigating the latent space, the VAE can generate synthetic customer profiles with realistic purchase behaviors, allowing us to test and refine recommendation systems without relying on real customer data.

Chapter 6: Building and Training Generative Models for Synthetic Data

Now that you understand the core concepts of Generative Adversarial Networks (GANs) and Variational Autoencoders (VAEs), let's get hands-on! This chapter equips you with the practical knowledge to build and train your own generative models for creating synthetic data tailored to your specific needs.

Before We Begin: Data Preparation is Key

Just like any good artist needs quality materials, your generative model relies on well-prepared real-world data to learn from. Here's what you need to consider:

- **Data Cleaning:** Real-world data can be messy. Missing values, inconsistencies, and outliers can hinder your model's training. Techniques like data imputation, normalization, and anomaly detection come in handy to ensure your data is clean and ready for use.

- **Data Preprocessing:** Depending on your chosen model and data type, you might need to pre-process the data further. For example, if you're working with images for a GAN, you might need to resize them to a standard format.

Choosing the Right Tool for the Job: Model Selection

The type of generative model you choose depends on two key factors:

1. **Data Type:** Are you working with images, text, time series data, or something else? Different models are better suited for different data types.

2. **Level of Control:** How much control do you want over the generated data? VAEs offer more control over specific features within the

latent space, while GANs might provide a wider variety of synthetic data.

Example: If your goal is to generate realistic images of handwritten digits for training a handwriting recognition system, a GAN might be a good choice. It can learn the underlying patterns of digits and create new variations that resemble real handwritten characters.

Getting Started: A Practical Tutorial

Let's walk through a basic example to get you started. Imagine you want to use a pre-trained GAN model to generate synthetic images of handwritten digits for your project. Here's a simplified roadmap:

1. **Prepare Your Data:** Find a publicly available dataset of real handwritten digits. Preprocess the images by resizing them to a standard format.

2. **Choose a Pre-trained Model:** There are many pre-trained GAN models available online.

Select one specifically designed for image generation.

3. **Setting Up Your Environment:** Install the necessary libraries and frameworks (e.g., TensorFlow, PyTorch) to run your chosen pre-trained model.

4. **Loading the Model and Data:** Use code to load the pre-trained GAN model and your prepared dataset of handwritten digits.

5. **Generating Synthetic Data:** Use the model to generate new synthetic images of digits. You might be able to control certain aspects like the number of digits or specific variations.

Training Your Own Model (Optional):

This chapter primarily focuses on using pre-trained models for simplicity. However, if you're interested in training your own generative model from scratch, here's a brief overview:

- **Training Process:** The training process involves feeding your real-world data into the model and iteratively adjusting its internal parameters (weights and biases) to improve its ability to generate realistic synthetic data. This can be computationally intensive and requires careful selection of hyperparameters (learning rate, number of training epochs).

- **Evaluation Techniques:** How do you know if your model is doing well? We can use various techniques to evaluate the quality of the generated data. Visual inspection is a good starting point to see if the synthetic data resembles real data. Additionally, statistical metrics like Inception Score (for images) or FID (Fréchet Inception Distance) can quantify the similarity between the distributions of real and synthetic data.

Remember: This chapter provides a foundational understanding. As you delve deeper, you'll discover more advanced techniques and tools for building and training generative models for synthetic data creation.

Part 4: Working with Synthetic Data

Now that you have the knowledge to create synthetic data using Generative AI, this section dives into the crucial aspects of ensuring its quality and responsible use.

Chapter 7: Quality Assurance and Validation of Synthetic Data

Just like any tool, synthetic data needs careful evaluation before it can be used with confidence. This chapter explores how to ensure your synthetic data is statistically accurate and realistically reflects the real world.

- **Ensuring Statistical Fidelity:**

  - **Concept:** Synthetic data should statistically resemble the real data it aims to represent. This means the distribution of values, patterns, and relationships within the data should be similar.

- **Techniques:** We'll discuss various methods for checking statistical fidelity:

  - **Visual Inspection:** For images or text data, visually compare real and synthetic data to see if they have similar characteristics (e.g., color distribution for images).

  - **Statistical Tests:** Perform statistical tests like Kolmogorov-Smirnov test to compare the distributions of real and synthetic data for numerical features.

- **Realism and Generalizability:**

  - **Concept:** Even if statistically similar, synthetic data might not capture the full range of real-world variations.

  - **Techniques:** Strategies to enhance realism include:

    - **Data Augmentation:** Artificially modify existing real data (e.g., rotating images) to create a richer dataset for training the generative model.

    - **Domain-Specific Knowledge:** Incorporate domain knowledge (e.g., traffic patterns for self-driving cars) to

guide the generation process and

ensure realistic variations.

Chapter 8: Ethical Considerations and Legal Aspects

Synthetic data offers immense potential, but it's crucial to use it responsibly and ethically. This chapter explores these considerations:

- **Bias and Fairness in Synthetic Data:**

  - **Concept:** The generative model can inherit biases from the real-world data it's trained on.

  - **Mitigation Strategies:** Techniques to address bias include:

- **Debiasing Techniques:** Apply algorithms to identify and remove biases from the real-world data before feeding it to the generative model.

- **Diverse Training Data:** Ensure the real-world data used for training is diverse and representative of the target population.

- **Data Ownership and Usage Rights:**

  - **Concept:** Who owns the synthetic data generated by a model?

○ **Legal Considerations:** Understanding and addressing legal issues around data ownership and usage rights becomes important. This might involve considering factors like:

- **Licenses for pre-trained models:** If you use a pre-trained generative model, understand the license terms associated with its use and the synthetic data it generates.

- **Data privacy regulations:** Ensure your synthetic data generation process complies with relevant data privacy regulations, especially if it's based on anonymized real-world data.

Conclusion:

By understanding these quality assurance techniques and ethical considerations, you can ensure that your synthetic data is reliable, unbiased, and used responsibly to unlock the full potential of AI in your projects.

Part 5: The Future of Synthetic Data and Generative AI

This section dives into the exciting future of synthetic data and generative AI, exploring cutting-edge advancements and their potential impact.

Chapter 9: Emerging Trends and Advancements

The world of synthetic data is constantly evolving. Here, we'll explore some of the most promising developments:

- **Explainable AI for Synthetic Data Generation:**

  - **The Challenge:** Generative models, particularly complex ones like GANs, can be like black boxes. It's often difficult to understand how they arrive at the synthetic data they produce. This lack of transparency can raise concerns about bias or fairness in the generated data.

- **Enter Explainable AI (XAI):** XAI techniques aim to shed light on the decision-making process of generative models. Researchers are developing methods to:

  - Visualize the latent space of VAEs, allowing us to see how the model maps input data to generate new data points.

- Analyze the training process of GANs to identify potential biases or weaknesses.

- **Example:** Imagine a company using a GAN to generate synthetic customer profiles for training a loan approval model. XAI can be used to ensure the generated profiles aren't biased towards certain demographics, leading to unfair loan decisions.

- **Integration with Machine Learning Pipelines:**
  - The future lies in seamlessly integrating synthetic data generation into the overall machine learning workflow. This will

streamline development and improve AI model performance.

○ Here's how it works: Imagine building a system to predict customer churn. Traditionally, you'd need real customer data. Now, you can use a generative model to create synthetic customer profiles with varying churn probabilities. This allows you to train your machine learning model on a wider range of scenarios, leading to more accurate churn predictions.

Chapter 10: The Impact of Synthetic Data on AI Development

Synthetic data has the potential to revolutionize AI development in several ways:

- **Democratizing AI for Businesses and Researchers:**

- Traditionally, large, expensive real-world datasets were a barrier to entry for AI development. Synthetic data can change that.

- Here's the benefit: By generating their own data, smaller businesses and research groups can now participate in AI development. This fosters innovation and widens the pool of talent contributing to the field.

- **Case Study:** A recent study by [University] showed how a startup used synthetic data to train an AI model for predicting crop yield.

This allowed them to develop a solution for farmers in regions with limited historical data, demonstrating the power of synthetic data for real-world applications.

- **Building Trustworthy and Responsible AI Systems:**

  - While synthetic data offers numerous benefits, ethical considerations are crucial. We need to ensure:

- **Fairness:** The synthetic data and the models generating it should not perpetuate existing biases.

- **Transparency:** We should be able to understand how synthetic data is generated and used.

- **Scenario:** Imagine training a synthetic data model to generate images of people for a facial recognition system. It's vital to ensure the model doesn't generate faces that reinforce biases already present in facial

recognition technology.